An Uphill Climb

By Elliott Bobo

Dedication

This book is dedicated to everyone that has a desire to change, a desire to make a difference, to people that understand that if you are not a part of the solution then you are a part of the problem. People that can accept truth even when it brings conviction into their heart. It's dedicated to my wife (April Bobo), my children (Jawaski, Nicholas, Alexis) my mom and step-father (Mary & Ronnie Kennedy), my brother and sister (James & Veronica Bobo) and a host of aunts, uncles, cousins, and friends. Ken Black, Arthur Avant, My godmother Patricia Boyd, New Zion Church family and my Pastor Leemar Boyd. And last but not least my dad, my father, my role model James Bobo Sr., the one who struggled so many days to make a way for his kids, the one that never gave up on me even when I had given up on myself. He was the one who seemed to always stand tall as a man with very little money but full of wisdom, honor, love, respect, trust, character and dignity. In loving memories of James Bobo Sr. (R.I.P.).

This book is about challenges of everyday life. The struggles of the poor communities, black families, problems in society, division among people, and division between God and Mankind. It may convict some but the intent is to inspire many, it reminds us of the things that we know and the things that we overlook. It reminds us of who we were, who we have become and what we could be. It reminds us that every choice has a consequence and we choose to take more time to think before making decisions. It reminds us that is our duty to be there for our children and die trying to lead them in the right direction. Last but not least, it shows us what happens when we take God out of the equation of life.

Dedication II

I dedicate this book to Laurel Rose Publishing for being such an outstanding company to work with. They are very professional and very inspirational when attempting to provide the service a customer desires. They will take your ideas and enhance them and will not make changes to your work but they will make suggestions to help. They listen to your vision and your passions, then they walk in your mind as they make your dreams a reality. Laurel Rose Publishing Company will motivate you to go to another level in life and to look forward to holding a product in your hand that you can be proud of. A product that you can say, "I wrote this book". They help you create greatness as well as obtaining a legacy to leave for generations to come.

Thanks Laurel Rose Publishing,

Elliott Bobo

Table of Contents

Forward

When I spent my first days years ago in Baton Rouge, Louisiana I had my first taste of the dish called Gumbo. It was delicious and very warm but soothing. I later found out that there were a lot of ingredients and time spent on making it just right. I never knew what was in it but I know that it's good.

I do know that my experience talking with Mr. Elliott Bobo that he also gave me my first taste of a dish called LIFE that has been soothing to my soul, emotions and outlook on life. I have been wanting and craving more and more of this delicious dish that seems to heal me mentally, physically, and spiritually.

I am so very excited that he was writing this book because I will use it in my daily life and now you can also. Just like my first taste of gumbo and my first taste of life, I can credit the Louisiana recipes and Officer Bobo's book for my soul being on fire.

Arthur Avant

"When you do the common things in life in an uncommon way, you will command the attention of the world."

George Washington Carver

Wake Up

In today's society we seem to be fighting a constant battle that we can never win. Because the fight is so tough, do we quit or do we keep fighting? We get frustrated, we get tired, we get disappointed, and disrespected mainly by our own race and family.

Most black communities only come together when something is given away for free, for a party, or at a club. It's hard to come together for strength to change.

What do I mean?

Think about the number of small black businesses that are producing the same product yet no one business has climaxed to its full potential nor has it really made the impact that it could have if it was combined with more resources, ideas, finances, support, and labor.

Look at the whites, Indian, Arabic, and Hispanics. They bind themselves together to climax one business to its full potential. Then they branch out to create and open a franchise of stores which are still owned by the whole group and not one person.

See, this makes it hard to fail, hard to go bankrupt, hard to become arrogant, selfish, prideful, or stressed because you are not in it alone.

Think about it, you see small communities with 10,000 people or less and half the population is black. You will find 8 to 10 barbershops and 8 to 10 back-porch barbershops. If you do the math it would be more profit if we combine. We would save and profit more together than on your own.

Even the churches today, on every corner there is a church or a church being built. You would think with so many churches there should be more change, but instead it's more crime, more rape, more dishonesty, more killing, more hatred, theft, and people dying spiritually lost.

We ignore combining, we ignore change, and keep bringing up excuses like *"The Man"* or *"White Folk"* get us down. Let the truth be told, the "White Man" don't make blacks steal, kill, or destroy. The "White Man" doesn't force alcohol in our veins, they don't make us smoke marijuana, snort cocaine, cook meth, or inject heroin in our veins.

"White Men" don't make blacks drop out of school, join gangs, or kill for material gain or respect.

"White Men" don't make you disrespect your parents or authority.

WE choose to live certain ways and get mad because some people won't accept it.

We publicly display our ignorance until it has become entertainment again. Yes, I said again! Years ago we were known as "coons" or "spooks" and were put in shows with extra black faces, red or pink lips, huge bucked eyes, and afraid of our own shadow.

Now it's BET, BET has stupid rap videos, music that degrades our mothers, sisters, aunts, and grandparents by telling lies and made-up stories portraying our women as property, trash, dirty whore, one night stands, a piece of meat, or just an easy quick shot with no strings attached.

So we are buying lies and stupid ways of thinking, just to make someone else rich. While not realizing that it's going to destroy us along with our children.

Catered For Destruction

Has anyone taken time to see that the corner stores have catered to our black generation? These stores sale everything a thug could ever want. These stores have marijuana pipes, grinder, drug concealment containers, swisher sweet cigars, cigarettes, top papers, hampers, Playboy books, pornography videos, alcohol, huge bling necklaces, watches, rings, earrings, long t-shirts, hoodies, ball caps, and rap music. Drug dealers are allowed to sale drugs on the property as long as they don't block the front entrance.

Have we noticed?

Have we noticed even on the Christian side? Tyler Perry got rich by putting our Christian ignorance on film. So now the whole world can pay to see and laugh at us shacking up, committing adultery, fornication, lying, gossiping, back-biting, and degrading one another with a bible in our hand.

We use God like an umbrella, only pulling Him out when it rains. God is our backup plan. When we can't get it done then we pray, call on God, or go to church.

Churches, pawn shops, and liquor stores on every corner and black communities are going to Hell in a handbasket.

And what is said?

We see it and we don't care. Pastors looking for prosperity, fame, and a large congregation to make a couple hundred thousand a year, and drive very expensive cars while congregations struggle living in poverty. They may say amen and shout on Sunday, but if truth be told most congregations don't understand the story of Noah's Ark.

Parents having kids so young that they grow up and live in the house like sisters and brothers. What else can you expect when a 12 year old has a child? By the time she understands what happened, she will be playing basketball, Uno, dolls or video games with her child and enjoying it like two children being friends instead of parent and child. It is a sad truth.

Think About It

Think about it, if the human brain fully develops at age of 27, what can a 12 year old do with or for a newborn baby.

We have turned so far away from God that we have forgotten what being a Christian is really all about. We have put Jesus and holiness out of our house as well as church. So now we are going nowhere fast and it seems like no one can see it except Tyler Perry, and we are paying for it one ticket, and one dvd at a time. We would rather pay someone to help us laugh at ourselves instead of changing.

Tyler Perry's stories tell the truth, but what good is truth if truth doesn't cause change? Almost like medicine that you need but you refuse to take it or to be hungry with a full course meal in front of you and you refuse to eat.

Now, let's turn the tables and imagine if we could put down our titles of Doctor, Bishop, Apostle, Elder, Evangelist, Prophet, Pastor and get rid of Baptist, Methodist, Seventh Day, Church of God, Church of Christ, and even do away with 15 store front churches, and all small old churches with 8 members struggling to send in dues to the headquarters that you never see and come together to have a great worship center. It would bring more people together, more ideas, sermons, and more finances together.

Imagine what change could happen with a mega Christian center with classes on marriage, divorce, child care, parenting, dress code, respect, hygiene, church ethics, tutoring, exercise, weight lifting, gymnasium with swim classes, ministry courses that offer degrees, etc.

I know it sounds good and it would be nice but it also is an uphill climb.

It's an uphill climb because black America has the crab mentality. I remember as a child the larger nice grocery store in the Southaven-Memphis area had huge tanks filled with crabs without a top on the tank because every time one crab got close to the top another one would pull the one at the top back down. It's crazy to not understand if you help one out, he then can assist all of us but we are so jealous that we would rather stay trapped.

Trapped

Blacks have gotten that enslaved mentality so bad that they are now like the story of the trained fish. A man had a fish that he placed into a 5 gallon glass container, and he then placed the container in the ocean. Day after day the fish would swim so fast until he slammed his face into the wall of the container. Whether he swam East, West, South, or North he got the same results. After a month of failure the fish learned his boundaries. So now he sits and watches all the other creatures swimming, playing, and enjoying the ocean. The fish admire them but knew that it never could be him.

So, the beginning of the second month, the man removed the container and the fish swam a few inches and turn and swim in another direction. All though the barriers have been removed the fish had been systemized, enslaved in its own mind that he can't do better and can't go any further in life.

Our young black men today live this way and also raise children to live the same way. We teach them to sag their pants, use slang language, not comb their hair, not iron their clothes, wear hooded sweat shirts in the summertime, spoil them, don't give them any chores, but just give cell phones, tablets, computers, expensive clothes, money in their pocket, and cars with no morals or sense of direction.

Parents help enslave their children and help trap them in their own little world inside a mental glass container. So every day they see all the opportunities around them just like the fish, but when you know your boundaries and you've told yourself, your parents told you and your friends have told you that you can't and this is how it is, you never will succeed in anything positive. They live life blaming the white man. He "got us down" or the "system is set up for blacks to fail".

This is the common thug comment, yet we know that the world is full of successful blacks. We just tend to look over them or call them "Uncle Tom Niggas". Blacks are so jealous hearted and lazy that most have accepted nothingness as normal. Think about how many of us receive government assistance. We get food stamps, or disability when we really don't need it. Thousands of us think we are pimping the system, but we really are crippling America and waiting on judgment from God. Because you are sorry to get assistance to pay your bills and then waste your check on drugs or lose it at the casino.

It's sorry to receive a disability check and make $40,000 yearly of untaxed money working jobs for cash. It's sorry to get food stamps and go and sale them for cash cheaper than its value just to get high, get your nails done, hair done, buy drugs, alcohol, or have a big house party. Single black women market children to increase the amount of government assistance just to keep from working. They also get low income housing and never get married so they can continue to have a live in boyfriend that's not on the lease so they can continue to pay $10 a month rent yet leave home looking like a movie star all while the kids look homeless, snotty noses, barefooted and babysat by the oldest child.

This is why a lot of times your daughters don't know how to be a woman. They know how to get pregnant, pimp the system, and sometimes get raped by one of their mother's boyfriends or night customers.

The Sad Truth

I've seen many cases where a little girl gets raped or gets pregnant by the mother's boyfriend. It is the parent's responsibility to keep their children in a safe environment at all times. If you are not working, how can you be too busy that you can't teach, how can you be too busy that you can't teach, spend time and take care of your children. We get angry when someone harms our child, we want to know what, when, where, how, and what's going to be done about it, but the real question is "where were you" mother or father?

Why are we absent yet angry? If you're not involved you don't have a voice. Sorry people's opinions don't tend to matter because people don't respect or listen because the hard working taxpayer feels that the sorry person is robbing them while they take care of them every day. They go to work and get endless amounts of taxes taken from their check and still come home and take care of their family without an excuse.

We need to understand that government assistance is supposed to be temporary help not a lifelong crutch to hinder people from becoming responsible and standing on their own two feet. Too much help for too long hurts people. It robs them of good character, morals, work ethics, or the concern of others. Free has become blacks worst enemy. We see our people do crazy things that seem free and easy. We think that we are getting over but really getting under.

Why can't we realize everything free still costs somebody? We will stand in line for things we don't want or need as long as it's free. But we don't like to stand in line for applications, to enroll in college, to vote, or donate money or time to a good cause. It's strange how we love to receive things for free, but every time we are asked to do for others there's always a price because we always want to get paid.

Whether teaching, preaching, wedding ceremony, mentoring a child, taking a neighbor to work, or an elderly neighbor to the grocery store. We want to get paid.

This is why this book is called "An Uphill Climb" because we have a long hard ways to go and it's not on level ground but uphill. Uphill has so much work involved in it and when we look into black America we see so much work to be done. It would be like having a

$300,000 house that's been framed up but has no doors, window, wiring, plumbing, or sheetrock and it's a week from winter time and you're almost out of money.

A painful picture of our future generation, they have been framed but there is still so much work left undone. Blacks were framed by Dr. King, Malcolm X, Marcus Garvey, Rosa Parks, Frederick Douglas, Harriet Tubman, Sojournal Truth, A. Philip Randolph, Mahalia Jackson, James Baldwin, Sarah Vaughn, Ida B. Wells, and Dick Gregory.

The foundation is laid but we have run out of volunteers to continue to build on what our forefathers started. The sad part is that we are not out of resources or material. We ran out of love, compassion, consideration, adoration, determination, exultation, anticipation, and sincere concern for our children.

Anthony Hamilton has a song entitled "Ain't Nobody Worryin'". In the song he says: nobody's worryin' when shots fly high and sirens start to rang! Ain't nobody worryin' when kids die young and mothers are suffering! Ain't nobody prayin' and when they kneel down low, they tie their shoe strings cause ain't nobody worryin'.

He is trying to tell black folks that we are sitting idle watching our kids kill each other in gang violence. The ambulances or the police cars are constantly blazing through our neighborhood and nobody seems to care and nobody is kneeling down to pray anymore. The only time we kneel down in the hood is when we tie our shoe strings!

Later in the song he tells us that when kids are young these are the precious times but diseases are taking lives while Medicaid runs out. He says: show me a welfare line, there is gonna be a mother on her own tryin' to be a drought.

But "Ain't Nobody Worryin'".

We need to understand that between poverty, racism, murder, rape, gang violence, unemployment, diseases, rare unheard of viruses, teachers that work for only a paycheck, corrupt police, crooked lawyers and judges, life can be very stressful. That one thing that we neglect is a true relationship with Jesus Christ.

Truly receiving Christ gives you his Holy Spirit that will lead and guide you. It is what really gives us hope. Think about it during the time of slavery. Black people, Monday-Saturday, were beat, raped, called a nigga, or boy and viewed as nothing. On Sunday morning, they were somebody! They were somebody even without education, without being able to read, without having any freedom, without having a voice in world they were forced to build. Yet on Sunday morning, they were somebodies.

They were somebody who was cared for, loved, and shielded by Jesus Christ and the love they had for each other.

Can you see them walking down a dusty, gravel road, humming, singing, and skipping because for one day they were free? Almost like God allowed them to see what Heaven would feel like one day when he finally calls them home away from a world of evil and hatred.

Sunday morning with Jesus Christ was the only hope they had, so they did whatever it took to make sure Sunday wasn't taken away. And today, Sunday is not important because it's stay home and rest, go fishing, wax our cars, or have football day with the guys, volunteer to work at our jobs to make double the regular pay.

Church today is only important to have a wedding, funeral, or we get very sick then church becomes important until the problem is over and then we go back to our old selves.

We have become modern day children of Israel. We were angry and frustrated being a slave in Egypt. God sent Moses to force Pharaoh to let us go and as soon as you get out and have one bad day you want to kill Moses just to go back to Egypt to be a slave.

Comparing God's bread from Heaven with Pharaoh's fish and spices, they came to a conclusion that even though they were beat and mistreated as slaves at least they got full daily. Yet God offered freedom, peace, Angel food day by day and a land of milk and honey if they could just continue to be faithful and obey.

This is no different from today: We have several government programs, several grant programs, several military programs but we don't have time to apply. We would rather get a body full of tattoos, body piercing, sag our pants, not shave, not comb our hair, sell drugs, break in houses or cars, and join gangs. We rather have babies that we can't take care of, live off of our parents while stealing from them, go to jail for stupid reasons and get mad because nobody wants to bond you out.

With this mind set we look down on what's decent, we look down on being educated. We laugh and degrade other blacks that are smart, we make smart not cool and discourage those that try. We say being smart and using proper grammar is acting "white" as to say: blacks are supposed to look stupid, act stupid, talk stupid, dress stupid and be stupid.

We can't deny it because we pick up habits and fashion from BET, movie stars, rap stars, or sport stars but we fail to realize that these people are rich. And when you are rich you can afford to look like a fool but you can't afford to look like a fool because you have to fill out applications and go on interviews but who's going to hire you looking like a fool?

Who will allow you to run their business with tattoos on your face and neck, eye ring, nose ring, tongue ring, clothes that are 3-sizes too big and a nappy Mohawk haircut, who? Then we get mad and called the people racist because they wouldn't give you a job, so now this is your excuse to steal, sell drugs or stand on the corner everyday cause the white man got you down and they won't hire nothing but white folk and brown nosing niggas. We love to blame others instead of looking in the mirror and meeting the standards of achieving success.

How can we be so ignorant to think the people on the movies and rap videos are real, don't we understand that the industry portray what sales to make money. Most entertainers have degrees, a college education, acting classes and a good background. They have limo drivers, nice suits, square toe shoes, cuff links, neck ties, over coats and maids. Yet all we own are a couple of pit-bulls, a pack of cigarettes, no diploma, your boys and a rap cd you made at home and you want to be like somebody that's not even real. These people are doing their job.

Think about if these rappers were real, why are they not in jail or in prison? Listen, if I was a gangster, drug dealer, who prostitutes women, steal cars, do drive-bys, and kill for fun, why would I record it and allow the whole world access to all my self-incriminating evidence that all the lawyers, judges and victims of our crimes to have access.

So if it's real, they would be in jail because it would be an open and shut case, all the evidence is recorded, your name and picture are on the cover so you can't deny it. Our ignorance is making other folks rich. So why can't black America wake up and see that we are living in a trap, a trap set by ourselves and we act like we can't see it.

It's sad to be blind by choice because a lot of the situations we are in are because of the choices that we have made. We uplift the image of "Thug Life" as if it really has made a positive impact on our culture or society. Why stereotype yourself and get mad because somebody treats you according to your attitude and appearance. We say people shouldn't judge books by their cover but we've been doing that for years. For example how did you pick out a girlfriend or boyfriend, husband or a wife without judging the book by its cover.

Yes, you judge the book by its cover because you never know or understand your spouse until 5 to 10 years after you say "I do" but you trusted the book by its cover. Many people will purchase this book because of its cover and will read this book to better understand the cover and understand the title.

It takes a few chapters to understand the cover and it's just like life, it takes a few chapters to understand life as well as people. So when you act like a thug, you get treated like a thug. You act like a civilized human, it's a 90% chance you will get treated like a civilized human.

Yet, instead of changing we always like to use the race card. But I ask this one question when, when was the last time the KKK dragged a family member of yours out of their house and hanged them? When was the last time the KKK burned your house or just burned a cross in your yard? I'm not saying that they don't exist anymore because obviously they still exist but we have taken their place. We have a new-age KKK, the black KKK, the thug life KKK. So we forced the white sheets to retire and activated the pants sagging, hood wearing, nappy headed, unemployed, love to get high, can't stand to see you do good in life group of people who kill each other. Every 30 minutes somewhere in America a brother is laying in a pool of his own blood.

Black life has as much value as a used piece of toilet tissue. We are getting killed for stepping on someone else's foot, bump into someone in a crowd, $5 in a dice game, because of the way someone wears his ball cap, because someone is in a different gang, turf wars, losing the basketball game, football game, or losing a video game and it turned into an argument.

The Truth of the Matter

It's an uphill climb!

It's an uphill climb because it's hard being black, trying to fight racism, jealousy, envy, backbiting, lying-haters, while at the same time we fight against each other. Dr. Martin Luther King died for all people to be treated equal and for all to love and get along with one another but we can't get along with each other. We can't get along with the people in our own household.

Children today disrespect, hit and curse their parents with no remorse. Parents today are afraid of their children, intimidated by the fear of what their child might do to them, afraid of what others would say if they knew what goes on in their homes. So now parents live like puppets controlled by their children. Adult kill themselves to make kids happy at all times.

Adults compromise with their beliefs and values to please their kids. Parents get depressed and broke because they are trying to please their kids only to get hit or screamed at because they took too long to get what the child asked for. Adults today are so weak that it is disgusting to hear children talk to their parents as well as the way they treat other authority figures.

This attitude had bled into the schools as well as the church. So now we are sending an angry, ignorant, thuggish, selfish, disrespecting child to school for the school to babysit for 8 hours but while the child is at school, he or she gets in trouble.

The school calls to have a conference to resolve the issue but the parent comes to the school wanting to fight the teacher and defend the child. Why would you defend a child that you know has always been a problem and you know the same way the child acts at home, the child acts the same way at school.

So there is no need to get angry at the teacher when you should be angry at yourself. I'm tired of watching senseless interviews about what needs to be done to correct the problem with teenage violence, troubled teens and drop outs. Spending millions of dollars on recreational centers and after school programs will not solve the problem, it will just give kids more to abuse.

Providing more stuff for kids without respect and responsible parents will just be more property for these wild children to destroy. We need to combine our resources and ideas to create programs to reform and inform parents, to teach parents how to take responsibility for the children that they birth into this world. Because if not children will continue to be neglected by their parent, left home alone to do what they please.

Children are being raised by music, movies, friends, homosexuals, pimps, drug dealers and the local gang. All this is going while parents are too busy to spend time with their child, too busy to go to the park, too busy to roll or bounce a ball, too busy to read a Bible story, too busy to show up a band concert, too busy to go to a ballgame or just lay in the floor and watch cartoons with your child.

We live in a society that thinks money can solve all problems. This is why kids are sorry and spoiled. Parents buy i-Phones, i-Pads, i-Pods, expensive cars, expensive clothes, jewelry, and even give large amounts of allowance hoping that this will keep the kids occupied so the parents don't have to spend time raising their kids.

All of this technology and no parental guidance give the kids freedom to learn about drugs, sex, oral sex, crazy fashions, how to get high on household products, how to prepare and use drugs without dying or getting sick. But what is strange is when your child gets pregnant, overdoses, commits suicide, goes to jail, rapes somebody, or steals. Then we have anxiety attacks, get depressed or act surprised that it happened.

Why not?

Why shouldn't it happen? They didn't know because they weren't taught and you weren't there. So until we are willing to treat the root why keep complaining about the rotten fruit that the tree keeps producing.

You can't get mad at the tree, but you can get mad at the roots and treat the soil. So take time to play with your kids, teach them, take them to church, pray with them, love them, raise them with the fear of God and the respect for authority. Visit their school, talk to the teachers, look in the classroom, show up at the PTA, volunteer at the school, help your school to help you raise your child and send them off to college.

Stop looking for excuses to cover up the truth that you're lazy and not really willing to work hard at being the person God created you to be. But you don't understand that your child is the one that suffers the most. I believe that anything can be an excuse but it's still not a reason. What I am saying is not 100% foolproof but if a child is raised in a real Christian family of holiness, great morals, trusts and believes in God and lives a life lead by love, it's a much smaller chance that the child will fail.

I did say *REAL* Christian homes of holiness, because the traditional black home is not real or holy. We go to church but we come home and get drunk, smoke wee, smoke crack, smoke cigarettes, beat our wives, have outside kids while cheating on our spouse and still say we are good Christian people.

We forget that our kids are watching us and hearing the people in the community talk about you. It's painful enough to know that your parent is whorish or to know that your parent is a homosexual. It's even worse to hear somebody gossiping about it in public. It's hard enough to know your parent is a homosexual or whorish around town but it's worse when their classmates are talking about it at school.

Real Parenting

If you truly want to attempt to change our youth then do so by starting with the parents, or our parenting skills. Look back at what parents used to be: compassionate, loving, and concerned. Parents that had time for the kids, time to hug, hold and talk to their kids were far more effective at raising them. But today parents are so busy that kids are not used to being hugged, held or getting a kiss on the head…they think it's gross or embarrassing because they weren't being raised that way.

This is because the home has changed. Think about it, kids back in the day didn't have a house key. When you came home someone was there waiting on you when you got home. A meal was in the kitchen even if it was a small amount of leftovers.

But children today don't eat leftovers, don't eat fruit or vegetables and don't drink water. They have a key to the house, no one is there waiting on them and no food is there for them to eat. Today it's, come home when you get ready and if you're hungry cook some noodles and momma will bring some McDonald's home whenever she comes home.

But what happened to the real home? What happened to the home where the whole family ate dinner together? What happened to the home where the family prayed together at night and blessed the kids before they got on the school bus? What happened to the home where everybody went to church on Sunday morning? What happened to the home where you ate what was on the plate or went to bed hungry?

Now we have so many choices, either parents stop at three different restaurants or have to go home and cook three different meals in an attempt to please all the kids. Parents don't understand that all they are doing is teaching the kids that no is unacceptable, you should always have your way, get what you want, when and how you want it.

So if you raise your child this way why does it surprise you when your child curses, fights, have anger problems, hit you, rape someone, get kicked out of school or go to jail because you have taught them to not accept no and to always get their way? Today parents are creating time-bombs, place them in society and hide their hands.

Take time and look back at how great children used to be. Think of how beautiful it was to hear yes ma'am and no ma'am. Think how beautiful it was to see girls fully covered and boys with clothes on that fit with a belt on and has a nice haircut.

Young America calls this type of life old-fashioned. They say that the Little House on the Prairie or The Cosby Show lifestyle. But it's amazing when these hardcore self-made gangster kids get sick or go to jail they tend to want love, hugs, kisses, and even prayer. Children today are destroying themselves with the help of their parents and the corruption of society.

Foolish Lifestyles

Think about this: you can't tell the girls from the boys because they all have the same hair styles, sagging pants, earrings in both ears, contacts in their eyes and they all try to act hardcore. So now we have to take time and look for breasts, Adam's apple or wait until they talk to attempt to identify what we are looking at.

If you choose to radically change your appearance and identity that draws negative attention and make you look like a suspect, why do you get offended by the way the common man looks at you or treats you. We fail to realize that the clean cut, well dressed briefcase carriers are not getting shot because someone feels threatened or because a bag of Skittles and a Coca-Cola looks like a gun.

I know it's not fair that blacks can't dress the way they want to dress without being viewed as a threat. I understand, but it is what it is! But if this is the world we live in why can't we adjust to it?

Number one, God didn't create a thug life so it really doesn't count when you say I have a right to wear what I want. True, but if it can get you killed, falsely accused or beat, why do it?

Think about it, if you woke up one morning and there was a snow blizzard outside and you want to wear short pants, flip flops and a tank top should you get mad because you got frost bite? Should you get mad because God let it snow or do you deal with it?

Dealing with it consists of dressing according to what's best for your wellbeing. Why can't we understand that the way it is is different from what you think it should be. It would make a little sense if you made money looking like a fool but you don't.

I would understand if looking like a fool helps you to get a job, degree or even scholarship but it doesn't. So what is the big deal unless you don't have plans to be successful. Most kids only have the same little simple ideas about life after high school. I'm going to play Pro basketball, football, be a rapper or, say if I go to college, I will major in mechanic or Heating & Air Conditioning.

This small mindset is to keep us down and at home in the hood with an excuse if it doesn't work out. Look in our community, look in the hospitals, doctor offices, court houses. Where are the black doctors, lawyers, judges, veterinarians, pediatricians, therapists? Where?

Every now and then we see maybe one but you won't know him because he won't be from your neighborhood. Because, our men are in jail, prison, on the street corner, the crack house, wanted for child support, or washing cars as his own self-employment.

We act like it's a sin to go to college for 4-8 years to establish a career. We act like it's a sin to go to work for a company and have set hours, pay taxes, and receive income tax while preparing for retirement. We act like it's a sin to work for minimum wage, to work for $8.50 an hour. We are too good for that stuff but we can stand on the corner for 14 hours a day and only make $40 but we don't have to punch a clock because you are self-employed.

Yeah right. You're a fool. How can you survive or take care of a family on maybe $40 every 14 hours? How?

But what's funny is these kinds of men are the one that nurses, secretaries, teachers, principals, judges are married to or dating. Why would someone work so hard to go to college for 4-8 years just to give all her hard work to a lazy thug that has been daydreaming of hitting it big one day that will never come? Why?

To add insult to injury they have kids that grow up in this environment thinking that this lifestyle is okay. So now the son is taught that he doesn't have to work, he just needs to find him a good whore with a good job, beat her up to keep her in check, hustle when you can, try to get home before it gets too late, and everything will be alright.

The daughter believes that she should get hit if her man is a real man and she needs a good job to keep the household together because her man will always be between jobs or out hustling. He will be angry when she can't give him what he needs until he gets up on something or wash another car, sell a cd, sell some dvds, or make a drug deal.

What is so attractive about an unemployed piece of nothing, women seem to think that they can fix up men like you do old cars. Just get a rough piece of nothing out of a junkyard and fix it up. Sorry, men don't change like old cars at a shop! But unless these women learn they will continue to marry a project and live in the projects also. Today it is portrayed that a hardworking, loving provider is too weak.

Real men of today's society has played out. Rough-thugged out men with no morals, unemployed, been to jail or prison, bad credit and cute is all that's needed. Women meet these type of guys on the internet and marry them while they are in jail or prison and wait for them to get out. Some marry guys that have 20 years to life, so every weekend it's family day at the prison so everybody can be together.

Some go so far as to get pregnant by someone serving life in prison and get mad if her family don't agree with her choice.

How long will we continue to live in slavery, yes slavery of modern times? If you live a life bound by bad credit, no education, no bank account, no career, in and out of jail, no ownership of property or business, just tattoos, earrings, bad hairstyles, violence, drugs and alcohol. That's modern day slavery, tattoos are your brand, earrings represent what slave tribe you belong to, your dress code tells what you represent, your hairstyle tells how much self-respect you have, your access shows how much hard work and management you have obtained.

It's bad to live in a place called the land of the free and we are not free. We are bound without shackles or handcuffs, just stupidity, ignorance, traditions, laziness, low self-esteem and no confidence in ourselves. When will we ever remove the wool from covering our eyes, we look at the news, we look in the jail and prison, we look in the church, we look outside and we even look in the mirror but still no change.

I read something one day that made a lot of sense. It said: ***It's not what you look at, it's what you see!***

We have been looking for years but we don't really see, think about it! If I see a person getting abused or taken advantage of and I ignore it that means I didn't really see it. When you see a need and meet it, when you see a problem you try to fix it.

Can we not see that black people are at the bottom of the food chain…but we are at the top of the list for drugs, crime, aids, government assistance, and incarceration rate. Can we not see that what happened to Emmit Till is still happening today? Can we not see that what happened to the Indians in Columbus Day is still happening today? Can we not see that we catch hell getting a business loan or a construction loan but foreigners come to the U.S. and receive a lump sum of money to get established, start a business and don't have to pay it back, just live here 5 to 7 years and it's okay yet we've been here all of our life?

Can we not see how foreigners can be trained on U.S. military bases and learn weaponry and how to fly planes then fly a couple of planes into the Trade Centers to show their appreciation? Can we not see that Wall Street pays fine while the hoods do time? Can we not see that the projects are never saturated with white people?

Can we not see that it's not normal to see a white family living in an apartment in the projects? Can we not see that the extremely wealthy pays less taxes than the poor average person? Can we not see that over 90% of starving people in this world are black? Can we not see that the government is killing us with the laboratory creatures, chickens fully grown in three weeks, seedless fruit grown in the normal time, extremely huge vegetables all pumped up with chemicals and steroids?

Can we not see that brain tumors, colon cancer, heart disease and etc. is the outcome of this fast money making system?

So, if you eat cancerous foods, smoke the government cigarettes, drink the government beer and liquor, smoke the government marijuana, and keep the tradition of eating the European slop bucket full of the slave diet? How do we expect to live and be healthy when most of us don't get enough rest, don't drink enough water, and we hate to exercise?

Can we not see this?

The system is set up for us to fail. Instead of telling you how to be healthy and live, the system just gives you quick fixes, pills, shakes, and energy drinks to help you feel good for a short time and later become dependent on a product that costs more than you really can afford to pay.

Listen, when Emmitt Till was killed his mother had an open casket, funeral, so the world could see how brutal this little small boy was brutally murdered. This sight was so bad that people fainted at the sight of this small innocent boy. My point is this, we live in this same society now but instead of seeing it for what it is, it's just like not looking in the casket at that funeral because of the fear of fainting or the fear of not being able to handle the sight of reality.

We are brutally looked over, frowned upon and mistreated and we still won't to join together to make a difference. Think about this, when have you ever saw any black officers on trial for murdering a white man or white child? But every time you turn on the television it is a white officer that shot or killed a black person with a 10% chance of being found guilty.

Because we are so intimidated by skin that black cops think a thousand times before shooting a white person but a white cop thinks after they shoot a black person. Black life is as valuable as a used baby diaper. If you can't understand what I meant by intimidated, listen, from slavery until today whites can hate blacks but will let blacks clean their homes, babysit their kids, and cook their foods without worry about blacks causing any problems because it's a proven fact that they know blacks are intimidated.

Think about it, a black cop drives through a black neighborhood and everybody continues to do what they are doing. But when a white cop drives through, kids run, people go in their houses, the whole scene changes because of fear. The big question is why are we so bold when we scandalized, hurt, raped, or killed our own but too afraid to stand against racism, go to college without being connected to sports or apply for a business loan.

The lifestyle we have created mixed with racism is a system designed to fail. But the sad part is most of us act like we like it. We laugh at the baby that says a curse word, we buy our kids gang related items and clothing, we buy our kids clothes and hat with marijuana leaves on them and feels that it's okay.

We buy our daughters low cut blouses, skirt that are too short and give them too much freedom and yet we feels that it's okay. When you find out your child is pregnant, in trouble, or in a gang why get mad when you're a part of the problem. Common sense tells you that your child just doesn't wake up one morning in love with wearing red clothes only, blue clothes only, or shoe strings in only one color.

It's not by chance that the group he or she suddenly loves to be with loves the same color clothes, shoes, hats or shoe strings. It's not a coincidence that your child smells like smoke and his or her eyes are frequently red. It's not a coincidence that your child suddenly eats more or sleeps more and is very angry and defensive.

There is a huge chance that your child has become a sexually active, weed smoking, thuggish gang related youngster. As a parent you can keep living blind, pretending not to see that you are losing your child. How can you watch your child slip away and you not do anything?

How can you not have a drop of compassion to want to see your child have a fighting chance to have a positive Godly life? I think most parents don't like to take out the time and make the sacrifice to meet the standard of being a real parent, a real example for and to your child. It may not be easy but it is possible and it is rewarding.

You may not receive a trophy, an academy award, or get recognized as a parent of the year. But you can see your child get saved, get baptized, graduate high school, finish college, begin a career, get married and have you some grandkids. But maybe that's not what you want for your child, you want your child to be a big drug dealer, convicted felon, crack-head or just a lazy 40 year old that won't move out of your house.

The Bible says that children are like arrows, and it's up to the parents to shoot them in the right direction. The Bible also says to train up a child in the way he should go and when he is old he will not depart from it. Meaning that parents should do all that they can to lead their children in the right direction.

Parents should be an example and role model at all times so they can have a pattern to go by and have a reminder when they have choices to make. When they are facing temptation or feel like giving up. It's up to us parents to be that difference maker.

If parents don't stand up and lead their children, society will lead them. Society will lead them straight to jail or Hell. Think about it, the government and the state makes a lot of money off of the prison system. If your children and your family getting in trouble makes the state and the government very wealthy why would they attempt to bring peace and lower the crime rate.

Have you ever saw a hospital or doctor's office sale books on natural organic cures? No because they would lose money. And the only gain would be less senseless killing, less children born out of wedlock, less drug usage, less shoplifting, less raping and robbing but peace and love don't make money. But alcohol, drugs, nappy head, baggy clothes, rap music makes lots of money.

Not only does it make money but it is addictive, causing our young people to want and look like what appears to be going on. So we are volunteering to cause our young nation, especially young black nation to be extinct or caged up in jail or prisons like animals we volunteered to become.

The reason I said volunteer is because it's not so much an issue of peer pressure today, it's a heart desire to want to look rough, to get in trouble and have a bad reputation. Kids are not forced into gangs that much now because they want to be in gangs. They want to be in gangs so bad that they create their own gangs, that's why we hear so many gang names we never heard before.

It is hard to encourage or convert a person that volunteers for a life of sin, crime and ungodliness. Because remorse, conviction, compassion or consideration won't exist in the heart of a volunteer because they chose to be that way. They desire to be the best at being that way. They have to have multiple sex partners, to have to have the wildest life styles.

They choose to be involved in homosexual and tri-sexual relationships and call it just being real. They choose to act vicious and silly so they can cause their parents to be afraid of them, and they can have their way all the time. Also to not receive punishment from their parents when they do wrong because the parents are afraid.

These children are manipulative and play their parents, police, teachers and counselors against each other. Playing the blame game and the "poor me" victim mentality. What this does is make all the people in authority positions to turn against each other while the child continues to do wrong. It causes some authority figures to feel sorry for the child and get used by the child. The adult will be trying to help the child and the child has no desire for change but will use the adult or authority figure to get what they want by acting like they are being helped yet pretend that it is so hard for them to change.

Without a true desire and want to change, how can you really be helped? So building a multi-million dollar youth facility will not change a community because if the children chose to be who they created themselves to be, all they will do is destroy the youth center or let it be the new place to meet, sell drugs, gang bang, gamble or fight over basketball games. We as adults keep on talking about doing what used to work back in the 80's and 90's but will have little effect now.

See, years ago people lived in poverty but they had morals, love, compassion and a father in the home that believed in going to church, praying, family dinners and respect. But now we have single parent homes with kids growing up with a parent that is an active gang banger that promotes hate, violence, alcohol, and drug usage. They are in homes that are full of sin and vulgar language.

Homes full of division and anger. Homes that hate the police, hate rules and regulations. Homes that feel like education is for rich white kids and hugs and love is for weak people. Homes that teach kids that they need $70 jeans, $180 tennis shoes, $60 shirts and $35 ball caps. Homes that say get what you want by any means necessary, rob, kill, steal, sell your body or pimp the government through EBT, tandem or false disability claims. Homes that kids are exposed to loud music, arguing, gambling, sex, drug selling, R-rated movies, shacking up, homosexuality, lying, gossiping, anger, disrespectfulness, ungodliness and no desire to have a real relationship with God and we keep talking about building a Youth Center when we need to focus on the parents.

Focusing on parents is the best approach, like catching alligators or snakes, the catcher does nothing until they get the head then they move to the next step. So my point is this: you can't attempt to teach positiveness to a child and then send him back to a negative home. It is like taking a good bath and go lay in the mud.

Why would I complain about my car going in the wrong direction when I'm the one steering the car? So why would you get mad at kids going in the wrong direction when they are steered by their parents or guardians?

I know that all homes are not like this because I know a small number of real parents that really try to raise their children correctly. But it is only a small percentage, possibly 10% of society. So the parents that are true Christians and really trying to steer their kids in the right direction is constantly catching hell. Catching hell because they have to allow their kids to go to school and be with and around the foolish kids that don't want to change.

It's scary to send your child out into the woods at night alone and woods are saturated with vicious wolves that don't care about anyone or anything but satisfying their appetite. So good kids have to keep their guards up at all times because it makes them want to become rebellious. Sometimes, especially when it seems like the foolish kids get all the attention while they only get a certificate and free breakfast for being an honor student.

If they are not very careful they will lose respect for doing good and end up becoming a wolf. Think about if they become a big bad wolf, they become popular, they think they will have respect because most kids would be afraid of them. Being a wolf would be exciting, full of thrills and chills from intimidating weak prey as they cry and run from them while being too afraid to tell on them.

So the kid now has become a bad boy figure and is finally getting the attention that he has been seeking for long. But so many times kids like this get in trouble trying to seek attention. In most cases they really desire attention from home and especially from the father who is maybe absent or too busy to spend time with them, too busy to love them and help them become mature enough to love and respect his peers.

The Power of a Father

A father in the home is so important that a child is robbed in this day and age if they are raised by the mother only. Any time after 1990 parenting has changed because discipline is watered down by teenage parents, rules and laws that give young or sorry parents an excuse not to discipline their children.

Notice I didn't say a male or a man but rather, "A Father" because based on the Bible "A Father" should be the greatest example for his children. He should leave an inheritance for his children, instill God's word in their hearts, provide food and shelter, pray with and for them. A father is supposed to love his wife like Christ loves the church.

America today fails to realize that without a father in the house your daughter doesn't know who to date or who to marry because she never had an example of what a real man should be. So she possibly will end up in love with some stupid looking thuggish dummy that don't want to work but only wants to control her and beat on her.

Where was her guidance, her example, where was her protector?

And your son without a father in the home robs him of learning how to become a man. He's robbed of learning how to love a woman and how to be faithful in a marriage. He's robbed of learning how to deal with bills, anxiety, depression, lust, puberty, poverty or just repairing things around the house. He's robbed of learning his heritage, robbed of knowing who he is and who he will become.

So, as a boy full of ignorance and yearning for the attention of a male figure to be in his life, he may steal, use drugs, join a gang or become gay. Becoming somebody that he's not may be harsh but he will get the attention, the hugs and kisses, the hand shakes, pats on his back, the "I love you", the "I'm here for you", and time spent with him. If a boy grows up this way he can handle jail or prison because to him it's no worse than what his house or the streets has already given to him.

So even in jail you still receive the attention that little boy deeply yearn for. Even if it's from inmates in his cell in jail, from the jailers and administration. Your family seems to care about them now, they visit, cry, hug them and even put money on your book.

You see, acting out in a child is a form of jealousy. See, in single parent homes there is nothing more painful than when a child is not getting any attention. If momma gets married or gets a boyfriend, the daughter gets angry because momma has been taken away from her.

No more riding, shopping, trying on dresses and shoes. No more laying on her lap talking about nothing while watching lifetime. No more hair done twice a week, no more nails and toes done to pass time away. So she acts out but too silly to admit that she's jealous. Too silly to except a father that's in the home and allow him to help them grow to become solid Christian adults.

At the same time the boy is angry too, because he misses the attention a little bit but most of his freedom and control is gone. He can't manipulate his mom to make her feel guilty about him not having a man in his life to do things with. So now with a father in the house there is discipline, structure, rules to follow, curfews, strength and dominance to deal with and most of all he has taken your mother and trying to run the house now.

So now there is friction in the house and mom is stuck between a rock and a hard place. To stand in the middle makes everybody mad, to stand with her husband makes the kids mad, to stand with the kids makes the husband mad and trying to make everybody happy makes mom depressed.

We have a lot of single women that can't or refuse to get married because it is so hard to do when you have kids, some have even decided to stay single and not consider getting married until all the children are in college just so she can dodge the challenge of making things work with a father in the home. Now she, as a woman, has robbed herself of stability, love, comfort, companionship, financial support and real Godly guidance for her children because it's not easy to deal with.

Why do we tend to neglect essentials in our lives when we know we need them but it is too hard to obtain and maintain? This is why people don't get married, why people rent houses, rent apartments, rent furniture, rent cars, live off welfare, child support and false cases of disability.

Spoiled

The end result of these single parent homes are 90% spoiled thugs. So basically single parents are buying love from their kids. Paying children hush money not to get on their nerves and spoiling the children in an attempt to fix the fact that there is no father in the household. We think that gifts are supposed to fix the problem but it only makes a child lazy, selfish, prideful, arrogant, and materialistic. Children then become hooked on expensive material things that they have never worked for.

It's to the point that the children compete with each other to see who can use their parent to get the most expensive shirts, shoes, belts, jackets, cell phones, earphones, caps and sometimes cars. But it is dangerous to raise kids that are not used to hard work, saving money, making due, appreciating what you have, contentment and being able to accept hearing "no" sometimes.

Children today don't know how to deal with the word "no" because they are spoiled. This is why we have seen kids killing their parents because they weren't allowed to use the car. We've seen numerous school shootings, a rise of teenage suicide, teenage rape, teenage depression. This is why schools have in-school suspension, alternative school, juvenile centers and teenage mental institute that are overcrowded because these kids can't handle hearing the word "no".

See, the real parent says "no", the police says "no", the teacher and the preacher says "no". So that's why the kids are so rebellious toward anybody who is in authority that is really trying to uphold Christianity, discipline or obedience. They don't obey or respect anybody that refuses to allow them to have their way all the time. So when these children of today's society finally hear you tell them "no" they get so viciously angry that they will hurt you and even kill you. Even if you are the police or their own biological parent because they want what they want, when they want it and how they want it or else.

We are raising and financially supporting domestic terrorists. We are creating walking time-bombs with low tolerance, no self-control, confused, ignorant Hell and prison candidates that hold their parents mentally hostage and in bondage by making them feel obligated to give them everything they can think of whether they need it or not.

It is sad for parents to think they are helping their kids when they really are hurting them. To help someone to better understand what I mean, let me share a story I once heard.

A littler girl found a cocoon. She took it home because she knew that one day it would produce a beautiful butterfly. She placed it in her room in a nice box with wood, leaves and other things from the woods. She waited for weeks and nothing happened. But one day she noticed that the cocoon was moving but the butterfly never could get out. After watching the cocoon constantly moving, she realized that the butterfly was struggling to get out, so the little girl tore a hole in the cocoon to help the butterfly to easily get out. After a few minutes of movement the butterfly came out but it was weak, fragile, and funny looking. Its wings were stuck to its back and not fully developed because it came out of the cocoon too early.

The little girl is like parents today that think they are helping but really are hurting because it was the struggle in the cocoon that makes the butterfly strong. It's the struggle that allows its wings to develop and it allows its body to fully develop and gain strength. So because parents spoil their children it causes them to not fully develop. It causes them to be weak, fragile, immature, not fully developed and not able to succeed in life.

Just like the butterfly that had to crawl the rest of his life, never being able to fly, we will have kids that never become respectable God-fearing adults that are able to strive and achieve success in life. All because their parents tore a hole in their cocoon because they couldn't handle watching their child struggle. So parents buy the expensive materials that kids don't need while never learning to cook, clean, wash, work, cut grass, iron or just say "no ma'am", "no sir", or "good morning" to be courteous.

Parents have crippled their children and helped corrupt society.

I'm not saying that all single parent household will end up this way but it is a known fact that the majority will. Also, I know that some homes with both parents in the home can turn out bad also but it's a very small chance. And it's also a known fact that most kids that are properly raised by both parents in a Christian home can turn away from how they were raised but it is a 80% chance they will come back to the teaching that was placed in them when they were growing up.

It's a biblical fact that if you train up a child in the way he should go and when he is old he will not depart from it. So only what's in you will come out of you. Why would you open a wine bottle and expect water to flow out? Why would you open a Sprite and Dr. Pepper comes out?

What I mean is this if you don't train your child and allow your child to disrespect you at home, how do you expect them to behave and be respectful in school or in the public if you didn't put it in them when they were small?

A Good Role Model

We let HBO, Cinemax, Glide, Twitter, Youtube, Facebook, Chatroom, Facetime, BET, the Local Gang and classmates train up our kids because we are too busy trying to be young again. Too busy trying to be a player or a cougar chasing after relationships with people that are your kids age, depending on Redbull, Viagra, hair dye and a lot of lies. Hoping to regain our youth and prove to ourselves and our friends that we still got it.

You can't regain what you never had, if you didn't get it when you were young, it's impossible to get it now. The only thing you will get is embarrassed, emotionally hurt, lose your money and look like a fool. And adults that live this way you fail to understand that you are lost and confused because as an adult you should be satisfied with where you are in life and how things turned out.

You should be settled and prepared to share your seasoned wisdom to help the younger generation understand what life is all about and teach them how to deal with it.

This can't happen if momma and grandma is at the club every weekend. Wearing loud color hair, long eye lashes, 6 inch high heels, mini skirt and looking for a boyfriend that's 30 years younger than she is.

The only thing worse is a rundown old man trying to keep up with some little girl that went to school with his grandkids. He got his hair braided, got on his cool clothes and a pair of Jordan's on his feet, fooling his self to believe he still got it going on while his son is somewhere lost and don't care because his daddy wasn't there to raise him.

At least that's what his son says the reason is, he had to blame somebody and his anger and frustration said blame your no good dead-beat daddy that's somewhere taking care of a house full of kids that's not his and giving all his money to a young girl that has no love or personal concern about his wellbeing. He's like dogs that chase cars, if he caught the care he can't do nothing but get hurt.

If kids aren't growing up with positive role models, how do we expect them to turn out good? Especially when they have no sense of direction. That can't get it at most of their schools because most teachers are working strictly for a paycheck.

Think about it, if teachers are working only for a paycheck how could they ever be a role model for the child? Children can feel love and passion from teachers that really care. This is why kids always have a favorite teacher every year that they attend school. But one good teacher out of every five that you meet is not good for the development of our kids.

See, love and passion gives real teachers patience and compassion that leads to helping a child instead of a suspension, a write-up, or looked down on as one most likely not to succeed. Why? Because, kids with problems messes up your day if you are a teacher working for a paycheck because you don't clock in each day to help, you clock in for a paycheck.

Working for a paycheck is on an all-time high. It is seen in all job fields and it causes a domino effect on positive outcomes of communities and children. See, this is how it works, when a positive person works with a lot of negative people it rubs off on the positive person. Soon the positive one starts to complain about the boss, the jobs, the hour, the pay and what should and shouldn't be going on in the work place. Soon the work performance of the positive person goes down, work ethics change and soon may even be late for work some times.

So they use to have motivation, inspiration, dedication or concern about making a difference, now just making a pay check in spite of the fact that you don't really deserve it and has not helped anyone along the way. One adult can change the atmosphere of any job and one kid can change the atmosphere of any school or classroom.

Who is willing to step up and be that one, the one to smile and speak to everyone every morning, the one that holds the door for the other to walk through? Who will be that person to hug someone that looks depressed or appear to be having a bad day? Who will be the one to encourage everyone to get along and work together, the one who will diffuse the situation and try to help others to come to a mutual understanding?

See, stepping up means stepping out and stepping out a lot of times means you have to stand alone in hopes of maybe someone will join you. But most of all will everyone accept you and what your standing for. Today we live in a time where people like to agree with the majority and look down on the few that don't agree with the crowd. We have almost lost true leadership throughout the world because everybody wants to please somebody that may be popular, wealthy or seem to have great influence in the community.

The famous "it's not what you know but who you know, one hand washes the other" mindset is ruining our community. But the sad thing is that the children are watching, hearing and learning to be lazy and manipulate their way through life without having any desire to be a leader.

Leadership is not easy because it carries so much weight. The weight of responsibility, accountability, choices, decisions, creative ideas for progress and speak out even when it doesn't benefit yourself. It consists of guidance, direction, control, management, supervision and organization.

So, very few people want to step up and be a leader because it's hard and they know that as a real leader, people depend on you and hold you responsible for so much. They know to be a leader means that you have to be accountable for things that happen and for things that don't happen.

It's easier to stand in the shadows and give our opinion. Stand behind the curtain and give our thoughts, stand behind the curtain and complain yet not participate in striving to make things better. I believe if a person is not trying to be a part of the solution then they are a part of the problem.

You Can Either

You can either go around the world or let the world go
around you,
You can either sit and pout or get up and do what you do.
You can either live your passion or let your passion die
You can either come out and fight or drop to your knees
and cry.
You can either live to love or love to live,
You can either take what's not yours or give what you
have to give.
You can either have a positive attitude or an attitude that
is bad
You can either believe in yourself and not walk around
sad.
You can either live your dreams or let your dreams slip
away,
You can either live a life of misery or you can believe in
what you pray.

YOU CAN EITHER.
ARTHUR AVANT.

Change is Possible

In life today we need to learn to deal with the hardships and trials that come upon us. So many of us make excuses to justify why we don't put forth more effort in succeeding we make excuses for why we gave up or lose the ambition to change.

But how do you get to a point of not wanting to better yourself? Hard times and down falls are not the end of your story it all depends on how you accept it and how you use it to better yourself. I'm not writing this to sound educated or to just fill the spaces on these pages.

Listen, I was born with a problem called epileptic seizures. I would have these seizures at least twice a day, and I had to take medicine to try to help reduce the seizures. Along with that issue I was diagnosed with Hyper-tension and is now known as ADHD. While dealing with those issues I decided to race my brother home from my aunt's house across the street. I was hit by a car and it broke my leg in half and knocked the bone out of the lower part of my leg.

And to think it was hard to deal with those issues, we still had to deal with growing up poor. We started out with two families in a small block house with a tin roof. We had cardboard on the walls and plastic on the windows, beds in every room of the house, no bathroom, limited amount of running water, a wood burning heater and no privacy.

After we moved into a house of our own it was better but still limited of space because I had to share a bed with my brother, share clothes and shoes with my brother. We only had basic essentials and nothing fancy like brand name clothes and shoes. Rustler jeans, USA 900 shoes, a couple of shirts was our wardrobe that we had to share.

We didn't have a TV in every room, didn't have cable TV, didn't have 4-wheeler, go-cart, or bicycles just the basic important things. Feeding hogs, carrying water, using the bathroom in a bucket, or taking a bath in a number two tin tub was normal. Working in the garden, the bean fields, the pea fields, or hay fields was normal in the summer time.

As life went on, I always wanted to do better in my life. I used to dream of having a nice house and riding in a nice car. I used to dream of wearing a pair of Nike's or Adidas tennis shoes. I used to wonder how other people could afford those kinds of things. I can remember our washing machine, we had to fill it with water by hand, add washing powder and plug it up.

When the clothes finished we had to run the clothes through the rollers on the top of the washer to get the extra water out. Then we would hang the clothes on the clothes line until they dried. The first VCR that we got, my parents paid a monthly note on the VCR and the remote control had a chord, it wasn't wireless.

We lived very simple, we ate a lot of simple foods like potted meat, lunch meat, spam, oil-sausages, rabbit, squirrel, deer, hogs, hotcakes, Karo syrup, eggs, biscuits, molasses, fried green tomatoes and fried potatoes. Any of these foods would be combined daily to make a meal. Things were very simple and seemed to be appreciated more because it was all we had.

My parents worked very hard working people that believed in being honest, loving and treating people right. They done their best to raise us the best they could. I did good for a while but my attitude, hyper-tension and desire for a better life caused me to feel like I was missing a better side of life. I started acting silly a lot, my mom had to constantly discipline me, fuss at me and give me different punishments.

I eventually failed in school my fifth grade year, got back on track until a couple of years later and I saw that I was going to fail my 8th grade year and that's when I quit school. I had been working since I was 16 but somewhere along the lines I got fed up with that too and decided to see what the streets had to offer. I began hanging out with the rough crowd, the ones that were involved in a gang, selling drugs, stealing and using different drugs.

It seemed like it was a good thing to do because I got popular very fast and started making a lot of money. But while I was living life to the fullest, making money, wasting money and hadn't took time to think that prior to me becoming a somebody, I had gotten two girls pregnant and I guess I didn't take it seriously because I didn't have time to fool with no kids at the time.

My parents tried to stay in touch with the kids after they were born but I wasn't there for them at that time. It's amazing how the devil can fool you to think that you are above reality, above responsibility. So, I'm making money but I'm wasting it on clubs, women, cars, clothes, hotels, jewelry, gold teeth, drugs and alcohol instead of taking care of my kids.

As the world changed and everything around me changed, friends were dying, going to jail or prison, I started feeling like I probably would be next but I was going to do my thing until that time came. After several encounters with the police, getting arrested three times in three different counties, paying fines, getting my driver's license suspended and ended up being watched by the local sheriff department.

I started to see things crumbling all around me. Some of my boys went to prison, one got severely beaten, two got shot and one was murdered in his home four miles from where I was living. I knew that my time was getting near. So after four bad car accidents, an intense back injury, I still refused to change my lifestyle. But one day I left home with a large amount of drugs that I was going to sell but I kept feeling down on the inside that I didn't need to separate it or place it in separate bags. I kept feeling on edge, feeling like something wasn't right about that day.

After being out all day selling drugs, night came, me and a friend of mine was on our way back to the hood to our hang out spot. We stopped at the store to get beer and cigars to roll a blunt to smoke. When I went into the store and was walking down the aisle to the beer cooler I saw an unmarked vehicle approach my friend at his car in the parking lot. I then took the drugs out of my waistline but at that moment I heard a still voice inside say "It's time". I put the drugs back in my waistline and opened the cooler to get some beer but the moment I opened the cooler door, Narcotic Agents swarmed in pointing guns and grabbed me and took me outside near my friend. At that time I could still hear that small still voice saying "It's time".

After receiving a second drug charge, but luckily it was barely shy of being a felony charge, I was able to get out and go home that night. But on my way home I began to look back on all my hardships, pain, suffering, I thought about how good my parents were, I thought about the two kids I had but they didn't know me. I then thought about a friend of our family that always treated me good and he always invited me to visit his church because he had become a pastor.

I smoked weed that night and drank some beer but I told my friend Mitch that night while getting high that I was going to church that following Sunday morning. He laughed and said ain't nothing wrong with that. He laughed again and said you always want to talk about God when you get high. As strange as it sounds but it was true and sometimes I was listen to gospel music as well.

But Sunday morning came, I got up, smoked me some weed, took a shower, brushed my teeth, got dressed and me and my girlfriend, April, went to church. We walked in church and it seemed like everyone was so loving and happy. We found a seat, got comfortable and was enjoying testimony service, good gospel singing, people clapping and smiling while praising to God.

Soon the pastor came forth. Pastor Tracey Burton was preaching about the goodness of the lord and explaining how we go through hard times and struggles but we have to be patient and wait on the Lord to bring us out.

He said: *They that wait on the Lord shall renew their strength, mount up wings as eagles, run and not be weary, walk and not faint, wait on the Lord!*

I felt like I had been waiting on the Lord and I needed that strength to help me to know that God was real, to know Christianity was real and to understand that church was not a joke. I needed that strength to stop using drugs, alcohol, to stop being so evil, stop being so angry. I needed that strength to become a real man. After church was over we hugged the members. We were invited to come again and we left.

As I was driving down the road I began to cry and the more I cried the better I felt. I started crying so bad that I couldn't see the road, so I pulled off to the side of the road. The more I cried the better I felt, I cried so much that my shirt was wet from the tears.

My girlfriend (April) asked me what was wrong with me and I mumbled to her "you must not have been in church today", as I continued to cry. After a few minutes I started driving down the road again. I continued until I was approaching the beer store where I always bought my beer. I quickly turned into the parking lot, jumped out and went into the store to buy me something to drink.

I bought a quart of beer, a bottle of wine and a box of black & mild cigars. So on my way home I opened my beer and began drinking it but it didn't taste like it used to taste. As I got close to home I drank another big swallow of beer and it still tasted so strange so I threw the bottle out of the window. As I turned into the driveway I was angry because the store sold me a bad bottle of beer. So I decided to drink my wine while smoking me cigar so that I could calm down and relax. I opened the wine, then opened the cigars. I lit my cigar and, after taking several puffs, it didn't taste like the black & mild cigars that I was used to.

I took a large swallow of wine and it tasted awful, so I opened another cigar. I rolled it, adjusted the filter, lit it and now the second cigar didn't taste right. Now I'm angry and starting to curse and all of a sudden a thought came to my mind. When I was in that church service during the prayer time I asked God that if he really was real could he take the taste for drugs and alcohol away from me because I had become an addict.

I was trying to make something work in my life when I already asked God to remove it and then was getting angry without realizing that the power of God was working in my life. I was living so wild and sinful that I really didn't think God was strong enough to change me, so God had to show me how powerful he was by snapping his fingers and just snatched my habit out of my body and I almost missed an answered prayer.

From that day on I was able to go forward in life. I went back to that same church for a few more Sundays until I eventually joined. There were days that I thought I wanted to drink or smoke but God's spirit kept me under control. I would try to hang around my boys and they would be cursing, smoking weed, and drinking alcohol.

I refused to join them and they would laugh and say "OH! I guess you are a church boy now, yeah right, nigga you ain't gone change, you'll be back to normal in a few days because you ain't fooling nobody".

I continued to go to church three times a week. I could feel myself getting stronger and more curious about God. One Tuesday night at Bible class I asked the Pastor to marry myself and my girlfriend. He had a few counsel sessions with us and the next Sunday we got married after church was over. I later started teaching Sunday School and about six months later I began studying to become a deacon. After serving faithfully as a deacon for about 2 years I accepted my calling into the ministry and began preaching God's word. It was a challenge because I was still learning to be a husband because the only thing I knew was one night stands, back seat sex and hotel rooms for temporary excitement.

I was learning to be a father because I had recently begun to see that I needed to be in my kids life, so I had three new challenges in my life at one time. But I had a lot of support from my mother and father that helped me in so many ways, they kept the kids if I needed it and most of all talked with me and helped me deal with the changes in my life.

My father gave me a couple of suits, shoes and neckties to help me to keep going because they were so happy that the wild sinner child is living for God now. A lot of people couldn't believe it because I lived so wild and smoked weed and drank alcohol about 6 to 7 days a week, involved in gangs, sold drugs, getting in trouble with the law, stealing, lying, gambling and whoring around in the community and now he's a preacher.

Knowing me from the past made it hard for so many people I grew up with or hung around to believe that I was for real. They watch me constantly, questioned me, asked others what they thought about me but they all came to the same conclusion that it seemed like my life really had changed. The pressures from females, old friends, the thoughts of what the street life and attention I used to get, the pressure of missing me making large amounts of easy money.

I ended up working at Western Sizzlin waiting tables until I got a job at Wal-Mart until I got fired and later began working as a security guard. While working as a security guard I got approved to get a house built. It was a dream come true because it was God that worked it out because I had gotten turned down 3 times by mobile home companies because my credit was terrible. But God was opening doors in my life.

At the time the house was finished I had not made full time on my job so I brought home a little more than $325 every two weeks so it equaled about $650 a month and my house note was $550 a month and I couldn't miss a payment or be late or I would lose the possibility of getting a full mortgage on the house. The contract was for one year of perfect payments and that would be the beginning of better credit, a full mortgage and a life of responsibility.

I worked on cars, washed cars and helped anybody in need of help until I got into barber school. It lasted for about a year and I graduated and became licensed. I cut hair for a while on my own and house to house and later began working in the barbershop while continuing to work as a security guard. After juggling these two jobs and trying to make things work out my wife went to school and graduated from X-ray school so things would be better.

As I began to grow closer to the lord, I realized that working two jobs takes up a lot of home time, children time, rest and study time to prepare for church. Even though I finally had gotten full time at the security job I knew I didn't have a future there. I faithfully committed myself to the job and learned every area of the warehouse where I was working. I eventually moved up to assistant supervisor and worked that position for about a year when the supervisor quit and the company sent another guy to the warehouse for me to train him to be my boss, yet he didn't have a clue how to run the shifts at the warehouse that I had learned over a 5 year period.

I felt disrespected and very angry because I didn't miss days or call out at the last minute like other people. I came to work in the snow and on ice and worked the shift alone because no one else would come in because the weather was too bad. I even came to work with a fractured foot and all my job could do to show their appreciation was to send his assistant to talk to me and try to explain that I had been a great worker but I wasn't seasoned enough for the head supervisor position but they needed me to train the new hire to be the new supervisor.

I wanted to quit but the lord wouldn't let me leave. After a couple of months I had some friends that were police officers that said they knew I was a good worker and was doing good in the community and they said I should apply for a job at the police department. I eventually filled out an application but I didn't lie or try to make it impressive at all. For the question about stealing, drug use, alcohol abuse or have you ever been arrested, I put yes on all the questions.

I said there was no need to try and hide anything and it come up later and I get fired. And I thought if I put all this on my application, if they still hire me then I will know for sure it is God's plan for me to be a policeman. I used to hate the police because me and my boys always said the police was the enemy but we felt that way because we were always breaking the law. And now I'm trying to become what I always thought were low-down people that wanted to harm us or keep us in jail. But about two weeks later I got a call to come in for an interview.

I came in to be interviewed with the chief. He had all my paperwork on his desk. He looked at me and leaned back in his chair, took a deep breath as he threw his ink pen on the desk. He then says, "Elliott, out of all my days in law enforcement I have never seen a person be so honest on an application. I saw your files from the past, I've been told a lot of things by a few people but I respect honesty above all. Honest people are what this department needs and I think you can be a help to this department as well as this town. I think you will do good because I know your father, he's a good man and I have the highest respect for him. I'm going to give you a chance but this is your next step. I need you to write a paragraph on all these things that you've done that are bad and explain what, when, why and what was the outcome on the crimes and charges. I will present it to the board, you will have a final interview and that's it."

About a week later I was brought in and went through the final interview, was presented to the board, and I was hired. I then asked if I could have 2 weeks before I started so I could put in my 2 weeks notice at my security job. See, even though I was done wrong God wouldn't let me walk off the job to get back at the security company because of how they treated me. So I gave the company my 2 weeks notice, continued to do a good job while I had a brand new police uniform in my closet waiting on me to start a new career.

As I learned my job as well as learned the streets and all the policies and procedures I realized that as a policeman you really can help people. I saw that I could relate to people because I grew up poor, rough, and I dropped out of school, I've been in trouble with the law but I now had survived and spared to be a living testimony that God can do anything and also that all policemen are not corrupt.

I never hit a person, never made up false charges, never mistreated someone in spite of what crime they committed. But I did check on elderly people, walk-thru businesses and schools. I always tried to be social with people in the community as well as get involved with the kids. Sometimes as a policeman it makes you want to get out of character of a preacher but God always reminds me that I need to always be a light to a dark world in spite of what uniform I'm wearing because you can't be out evangelizing while you are at work but you can add Christ to every situation you deal with and add Christ in every decision you make on the job.

There are times as a police preacher I've had to sit with people and pray with them when they lose a loved one. It's not easy and God has to word your mouth and guard your heart. And other times I have to stand in the hood and not be nervous because I grew up in that type of environment plus I know what to expect and how to deal with.

I know a lot about drunk people, drug users, drug dealers and the everyday deceiver. So God allowed my past to become tools to help me in my future, it also gives me a passion to help because I can see where kids are as well as where they are headed, so they can be helped if they would just listen. But most kids have too much pride and are too weak to be themselves because they try to prove to their friends that they are hardcore and not afraid of anything.

It's sad that kids can be so ignorant and immature that they would waste their whole life trying to be what they think they need to be to satisfy the expectations of their peers based on what they see on television. What they fail to realize is that pleasing your friend doesn't give you scholarships to college. It doesn't get you high grade point average or good ACT scores. It doesn't give you a letter of recommendation. It doesn't pay the bills, buy cars, clothes or housing, the only think it gives you is temporary acceptance, stress, anxiety and a false lifestyle.

I can't understand how a broke unemployed, uneducated silly child tend to seem like he's so popular at school. But have you ever taken time to look at the big picture because these types of kids are only popular within their silly group. You can't put a fool in a room of intellectuals and he gained acceptance and popularity among the group because they are going somewhere in life and wouldn't have time for stupidity.

The only thing the fool knows is to act stupid. The fool knows how to make someone laugh or degrade the ones who are intelligent because he is so intimidated because he can't meet the standard. So instead of humbling himself, ask for help so he can make it through school and life. Instead the fool will start a fight to take his frustration out on the students he wishes he could become. But it's hard to do and he's embarrassed to try for fear of failure, plus his so-called cool crowd will find out and joke on him too bad.

That's why it is good to have made your mind up before you begin anything, that's why for years we've always heard that your first impression is the best and lasting impression. What that says to this generation today is if you be yourself from the start you would be accepted by those who are similar to you and will help you. Then you would have real friends because they can see the real you, love you, trust you, be there for you but the pretender is like a chameleon lizard, you change to be like whatever group, room or atmosphere to try to blend or fit in.

If something doesn't fit you don't force it, so why do kids try to force themselves to fit where they don't belong? Common sense should tell you that you don't belong so continue searching until you find where you need to be, not cry or get depressed because one group doesn't like you. It's not like that's the only group of people on the planet. That is why this book is titled "An Uphill Climb" because to climb is one thing but to climb uphill is even worse because the odds are against you.

Just like today's youth, they are so lost and caught up in Hollywood, BET, NFL, NBA, or the neighborhood drug dealer that they have caused the odds to be against them. So for real parents, preachers, teachers, policeman, or other authority figures it is an uphill climb to try to save these children from Hell, jail, prison, pregnancy, homosexuality, rape, molestation, drug abuse, alcohol abuse, depression, suicide or losing their mind.

Think about it, how do you save a person that's fighting against you? That's why there has been a time when people have tried to save people who were drowning but had to knock them out because they were fighting the one who was trying to save them and could cause them both to drown. So those that care has to fight the children, the world, the music, the movies, the media and this is nothing more than an uphill climb because the kids like what's killing them because they think they fit in. It's sad but true! It's an Uphill Climb!

The Cold Truth

Yes, dealing with today's society is an uphill climb because children as well as parents seems like they have lost the desire to become better, they have lost the desire to make a difference. It's like everybody is looking for the easy way, very few wants to deal with a challenge. Living life dodging anything that's not simple and easy. If they took time to look around they would see that they are traveling down a one way street that has a sign posted that says "dead end" but they keep going at a high rate of speed as if they are prepared for the crash at the end of the street.

It is sad to know that you're headed for destruction but too silly to turn around. I think some don't turn around because so many others are headed in the same direction, we have trained our minds to think that if a large crowd of people are involved in sometimes that means it's right. But this is the biggest distraction, the biggest illusion we ever believed.

We need to remember that the Bible says: the way to salvation would be narrow, straight and hard to find. And the road to destruction was broad, very wide, easy to find and many would be traveling on this path. Also it says that few people will find and travel on the narrow path. So we don't like to follow small crowds, small churches, small gatherings or deal with people that are not a part of the large crowd. So we have learned to go along to get along, we conform to the world to get along with the large crowd going down a dead end road.

Why are we so excited to go to Hell while talking about Heaven? Why are we so excited to say we are living for the Lord while serving Satan? That's why it's an uphill climb because we have parents that need to be reformed as well as kids that need to be reformed. We have children that want to be grown and we have grownups that want to be a child again. Adults today want to be friends with their children instead of being a parent and the only thing that comes out of parents trying to be friends with their kids is that the parents become very young grandparents, depression, stress, anxiety and another mouth to feed that you don't have room for.

Parents don't realize that they will be punished and judged for not raising their children properly. Because you conceived something, not manage it, then turn it loose in society to be a problem for others to deal with it. Listen, you would be no different than the people who buy pythons, alligators, tigers, and panthers because they thought it was cool to have one.

But as soon as the animal gets out of control these people become afraid of what they decided to obtain, so they turned them loose in the middle of the night and pretend it never happened. But what about the little baby that gets squeezed to death by the python, what about the old lady that gets eaten by the alligator, what about the little girl that gets eaten by the tiger, and what about the man attacked by the panther?

It may sound harsh but it is reality, because these unraised, misguided animals are like children, turned loose in society by parents that act like they don't know what happened. But who will give an account when they rob your mother, rape your sister, kill your brother, take advantage of your dad or molest your little brother…then what?

Who will we blame, how will you sleep that night, and what will you tell the family of the victim? What words will you use to help them understand that your child just made a mistake when he or she took the life of their loved one? Also tell me how do you replace someone's mother, father, sister, brother, grandparent or great-grandparent? How do you replace a human life that was taken because your child wanted to get high but didn't have any money? How do you mend broken hearts that were shattered because of senseless stupid teenage violence?

What happened to parents that controlled their house? When I was growing up we had to ask to go outside and we didn't leave the yard without permission. We had to eat what was put on our plate, there were no choices and if you were tough enough to voice your opinion you got slapped in the mouth.

We had a fear of our parents, we didn't talk back, we respected all adults and authority figures and we appreciated the little things in life. But now if parents don't make sure kids know their place they take their parent's place. I hear kids fussing at their parents, cursing their parents, some even tell them to shut up and now they call their parent "mane" instead of calling them by their name because "mane" is the new slang language.

But it's the parents fault for allowing their children to disrespect them so much. What happened to the strength of parents? I see parents that call the police to come to their house because they have a 12 year old that they say they can't do anything with the child, "he or she won't obey me".

What could possibly be inside a 12 year old that's so powerful that it would make a 35 year old adult afraid of them? And if you can't control one child why would you have five more that you can't control but get upset when they end up in trouble or talked harshly about you in your community? Until parents stop running the street, establish a real relationship with God, they will never be able to raise and lead their children in the right direction.

Unless parents walk with the Lord they can't positively influence their children to live solid lives. So until the parents surrender and become real leaders, how can you lead a child somewhere you have never been yourself?

When kids are able to see that you take God seriously and you follow God's guidelines then they can respect, understand and visually see what you are trying to teach them. It's simple, a lot of habits and attitudes come from home. Children often imitate what they see at home so parents should always be careful what they do in front of their kids.

You see, kids keep a track record, so you can tell them that it's wrong to do something and the next week or month you do. They will remember and do their best to remind you. Parents have to be mindful of this simply because kids need to see our integrity. All integrity means is that you need to be honest, truthful, a person of good morals and honor.

Godliness and integrity forces kids and adults to respect you regardless of what someone else may try to make them believe about you. It will be because your lifestyle speaks for itself, and your lifestyle speaks to your children. When it's time to discipline your kids they should understand why they got a whoopin' and should still love and respect you afterwards because you have raised them properly and to understand in life all choices have consequences. In short, don't make a choice if you can't handle the consequences.

I don't understand why it's so hard for kids to understand and accept consequences. How can animals understand this better than kids? Listen, I have a small house dog and when she was little and did something wrong I would lock her in her kennel. Her freedom and privilege to roam around the house was taken away because she broke the rules of my house. As she got older and would do something wrong I would call her in a different tone of voice and before I got through talking she would run out of the room. When I went to look for her she would be in her kennel laying down in the very back of the kennel because she knew she had done wrong.

Yet on the other hand I've seen elephants at the circus do tricks and then wait for peanuts. I've seen seals perform at Disneyworld and then wait for fish. So I say again, can an animal, a creature with no soul, have stronger conviction than a human that has a soul and made in the image of God but not have conviction or understand choices and consequences?

How?

How can animals over exceed humans? Think about it! You have never seen two boy dogs having sex. You have never seen two bulls in the field breeding. You've never seen two roosters getting it on but we see God's ultimate creation living backwards, living against the natural and normal order of God.

Listen, would you drink from a sewer drain? No! So why are so many men today loving the sewer drain of another man? Because animals have more morals, dignity, integrity, and self-respect than humans? How can we allow animals, a creature that licks its own butt, to live morally better than we do?

Yes, it's an uphill climb, a battle, a serious challenge, a hard pill to swallow, a fight with your back against the wall. It's tiresome because God's people don't have a lot of support. It's like fighting an unfair fight with the odds being 10 to 1 but you can't give up.

Going To The Next Level

In life there are so many people who are full of gifts, talents, and abilities. These types of people have become stuck in their comfort zone. Comfort Zones are places that are most times meant to be temporary but we get comfortable and make it our permanent dwelling place. So many stepping stones have become pillows to help get comfortable where we are in life.

We feel a need for MORE sometimes but we ignore that feeling because we fear the challenge of change. To help us understand what I mean I want to tell a story about a baby eagle that got lost and mix in with a group of chickens. As the baby eagle mingled and played with the baby chicken, it began to learn how to walk. It learned how to search for food and eat like chickens.

As the little eagle began to grow he noticed that he was outgrowing his family. He noticed he was bigger, stronger and seemed extremely different from his family. Even though he noticed that he continued to do his best to fit in. When the whole litter was fully grown the eagle realizes that his beak was larger, wings were longer, and his body was extremely larger than his family's.

One day he was in the yard eating insects, a large shadow covered the ground where he was standing. He began following and watching this creature. The more he studied this creature the more he began to study himself. He began to compare his face, his body, his wings to the creature that he had been watching. At that moment he realized that the feeling that he had down inside all those years were real. He realized those feelings were true, he was different. He realized there was more to life than the chicken coop, chicken yard or the farm where he grew up.

Watching the large eagle soaring through the sky allowed him to understand that the large wings he let drag across the ground was his ability to fly. And those years he and all the other chickens would run, flap their wings and glide to the top of the chicken pen and sit, when all the time down inside of him was the ability to fly and soar through the skies. He has been missing an opportunity to see the world. He was missing out on having his own family. He was living on the ground and in pens with chickens because he didn't know who he was or what he was.

It's sad to be an eagle and not know it. Especially when eagles are the top bird in the world. They are the largest bird with the largest wing span. They are the strongest bird and has the keenest eyesight. They are the only bird that can fly almost as high as an airplane and not die. No other bird can breathe at that height except for the eagle.

It's funny how we can cause ourselves to become trapped in life because of our small mindset, trapped because we never learned who we are or what we are so we never know what's down inside. Many people even die with so many gifts and talents trapped inside. It's amazing that the most wealthiest, talented and gifted place is the grave yard. Millions have died full of gifts, unspoken speeches, unwritten books or songs, unestablished businesses and even professional athletes; talents buried forever, untouched and undiscovered.

No one knew and no one ever will know because nobody ever motivated them to go to the next level in life. So millions lived trapped lives like an eagle among chickens, never knowing that all they ever needed was down on the inside. Although they knew they were different and they always felt there was more to life, they remained in their comfort zone, yet living in the comfort zone kept them from going to the next level.

I just wonder how many eagles are in their comfort zone with the chickens. These chickens can be mothers, fathers, sisters, brothers, or friends. We sometimes think that getting away from family and friends is a bad thing. Yet we fail to realize that all the years that you have dedicated your time and life to them very little progress has come out of it.

I've always believed that it's nothing wrong with hanging around or following people if they are going somewhere in life. But explain why we commit ourselves to people who are at a standstill in life. A chicken coop is not that big and you can only go in the same little square or circle for only so long. If the eagle stays among the chickens and always tells himself this is the way it's supposed to be.

My pastor has a saying that he always tells his congregation. He says: if you keep doing what you've been doing, you're going to keep getting what you've always gotten. In other words you can't expect to go to the next level in life if you want to hold on to your old way of life. In other words, why would a farmer constantly plant corn seeds and at harvest time he gets made because apple trees didn't grow. You will only get out of it what you put into it. If you change your ways then you can change your life.

New wine goes in a new wine skin. We want to mix new with the old. We want cake, ice cream and eat it too. Going to the next level consists of sacrifice. Sacrifice of family, friends, finances and times. Most of all remember it won't be easy because it's an uphill climb.

Equipment

Going to the next level is not easy because it is more of a mental battle than a physical battle. The Bible said, "be ye transformed by the renewal of your mind", meaning man can't change until man's mind changes. So it's very important how we see ourselves. Listen to this poem, it was George Washington Carver's favorite.

"You have ALL that the greatest of men have had!"

Equipment by Edgar A. Guest

Figure it out for yourself, my lad,

You've all that the greatest of men have had,

Two arms, two hands, two legs, two eyes

And a brain to use if you would be wise.

With this equipment they all began,

So start for the top and say, "I can."

Look them over, the wise and great

They take their food from a common plate,

And similar knives and forks they use,

With similar laces they tie their shoes.

The world considers them brave and smart,

But you've all they had when they made their start.

You can triumph and come to skill,

You can be great if you only will.

You're well equipped for what fight you choose,

You have legs and arms and a brain to use,

And the man who has risen great deeds to do

Began his life with no more than you.

You are the handicap you must face,

You are the one who must choose your place,

You must say where you want to go,

How much you will study the truth to know.

God has equipped you for life, but He

Lets you decide what you want to be.

Courage must come from the soul within,

The man must furnish the will to win.

So figure it out for yourself, my lad.

You were born with all the great have had,

With your equipment they all began,

Get hold of yourself and say : "I can."

I think this poem is his favorite because it takes a large amount of mental strength to excel in life. He was born a slave and was an orphan. In spite of this he educated himself, went to college and became the first black scientist, painter, and musician. He was the first to discover a mobile laboratory to teach slaves about crop rotation. He developed over 300 uses for peanuts, 100 uses for sweet potatoes. He developed and alternative fuel for cars out of soy beans and developed numerous other inventions.

This should inspire all of us to understand that we can live a life without limits if we believe, give our 110%, trust God, and never give up.

The sky is the limit, the battle is in the mind, and the greatest challenge is to conquer life's struggles. It's not easy, it's an uphill climb!

This book and its stories are very inspiring. This book makes you feel like making a change. It makes you feel like making a difference. It makes you feel like doing some things differently. Yet reading this book may make you feel good or make you feel fine. But when you get through reading, life is still an uphill climb!

Dying in Vain

We can't give up because even though Dr. King tried to make a difference for what he believes God put on his heart, we still are so far away. Listen, on February 4th, 1968 Dr. King preached a message called the drum "Major Instinct". He talked about people that live above their means, he said they drove Cadillacs and Chryslers but really couldn't afford a model T Ford.

He said this type of person lived in the $40-$50,000 houses but only made less than $10,000 a year. He said these types of people were always barely making it but wanted everyone to think they had it going on. He goes on to say: these type of people always talk about themselves, boasting and lying about what they got and who they know. Then he says: according to research of economics, no person should buy a vehicle that costs more than their yearly income nor should a person buy a house that's more than twice their yearly income.

But he was teaching people why they were struggling to make it.

It was amazing to me that what Dr. King saw 47 years ago is still going on today. People that want to be recognized, people that like attention, people that will go to any extreme to make themselves seem more that what they really are. He saw the evil hearts of those who were prejudiced and he saw the fear in the hearts of those who were too weak to stand together.

When will we ever wake up and realize that we are stuck in a rut, realize that we have so much more work to do? When will we realize that the struggle that we are entangled with is really an uphill climb? It's an uphill climb because today we live with an everyman for his self-mentality, an "I got mine you got yours" mentality.

But Dr. King lived every day for the sake of others, he got involved in the affairs of others. He tried to feed the poor, visit those in prison, he tried to bring peace, justice love and equality. He knew it would cost him his life because he always stated that it is good to live a long and pleasant life but that wasn't in his future. He many times preached that God had shown him the promise land even though he would not be able to go there with them.

He put others first because he had such a passion to see change for all mankind. A passion of love and unselfishness that eventually took him to his grave. Yet today we have nothing positive that we are willing to stand up for, to protest or march about. Today we accept any and everything, we go along to get along.

We die daily in numbers but not for a positive cause. Today we die in gang violence, suicides, senseless fights, we die over arguments in dice games, bets on football games, or bad drug deals. We die in adulterous relationships, we die from cocaine, alcohol, meth abuse, we die from robbery attempts. We live life foolishly and we die in vain. It's an uphill climb!

When I say live foolishly and die in vain I'm talking about people that live fast lives and don't have life insurance or burial insurance. The people that don't take life seriously and really don't care about their family enough to listen to anyone that tries to tell them to slow down, get rid of bad habits, get a job, get you some insurance but all they will do is get angry and say "I'm grown, this is my life, and I'm not hurting anybody but myself".

Yet as soon as they die the family has to grieve and raise money at the same time just to give this rebellious family member a decent funeral. To add insult to injury the unpaid debt and children that maybe left behind becomes another burden for the parents, the wife, girlfriend, cousins or other close relatives. But in reality this is a foolish way to live and a vain way to die.

It's foolish and vain to live a loose and worldly life but when you die all you leave behind is heartache, headache, debt, child support, multiple mothers or fathers. It's foolish and vain for a boy to grow up thinking that being grown means to be able to curse, drink beer and smoke cigarettes without getting in trouble. It's foolish for little girls to grow up thinking that being a woman means having a baby.

Instead we should strive to live a life of positive purpose, a life that glorifies God, uplift Jesus Christ the Savior and try to leave a lasting impact on your family, your neighborhood, even the whole world.

It brings tears to my eyes as I watch the youth of today living as if they don't understand their history. They act like they don't understand what it took for them to be where they are today. It brings tears to my eyes as I watch documentaries on racism and segregation of the past, the story of the Civil Rights student, Emmitt Till, or Dr. King's murder.

It brings tears to my eyes as I watched the movie "Selma" as it portrayed what happened in Selma Alabama while Dr. King attempted to bring equality to a harsh state. It brings tears to my eyes to watch thousands of our ancestors being disrespected, beat with whips, night sticks, shot, slapped, punched in the face, arrested, and robbed of rights and dignity. It was hard to watch the first scene of the Edmund Pettus Bridge of Selma's city limits. On the bridge hundreds had their skulls, spines, arms and ribs fractured while large groups cheered on those who caused harm.

Some of the same white people who were cheering for violence on the bridge, later that night beat two white men to death because they supported the march of Dr. King. Can you imagine what it took to be non-violent or to just live in a time when hatred was so vicious and publicly displayed? 60% of it is gone now, yet we have chosen today to torture, injure, and enslave ourselves and others instead of educating, and encouraging ourselves.

We can learn that courage, desire, hope, compassion and consistency can make a difference. Listen, all of the pain, torture and death in Selma was mainly for the right to vote but now that we have that right, the average citizen doesn't care to vote and a lot of times doesn't know who's running in the state or local election. It's amazing how we fight as long as we hear no and quit fighting after we hear a few "yes you cans".

I know I'm not perfect. I made more than enough mistakes. I wasn't always there for my kids. I wasn't always responsible. I've been arrested a few times, abused drugs and alcohol. I'd given up on life once upon a time but God spared me to have sensible baby momma, a loving wife, a caring mother and stepfather and most of all a relationship with Jesus.

So I sit in a pool of failure, along with an eighth grade education, writing a book in an attempt to give someone hope, desire, compassion, love, appreciation, justification, a chance, and a real dream. So don't view this book as an insult but rather a book of truthful constructive criticism. We simply needed to be reminded about the things that we've lost focus on. It's not easy but very hard. It's an uphill climb!

Never Give Up

By Arthur Avant

In the most impossible situation,

the possible is always there.

Never give up on anything,

no matter if you're trapped in a snare.

When you think there is no way

to turn the bad around,

find that reason to live

and plant your belief on solid ground.

Never give up no matter

The situation you are in.

Walk by faith, not by sight

Remember no one is free from sin.

Never give up when you have so much

To offer and give

The tears you may shed,

May be the nourishment you need to live.

Everything is possible,

If you never give up and see the light.

Never give up with, with God all things

Are possible, never give up and fight.

Afterward

After reading this book you can now understand that life is a journey of ups, downs, changes and turn arounds. It has a lot of valleys that we have to travel through. Most valleys are dark, dreary, confusing, and most of the time won't have anyone to walk along side you to comfort you until you come out. Life can be scary sometimes because it's so hard to understand the what, whens, and whys of yesterday, today, and tomorrow. There's nothing wrong with looking back at yesterday as long as you learn from them. Also, if we can appreciate our todays we can really look forward to seeing a tomorrow.

Life also has hills and mountains that are also hard to climb. Climbing hills and mountains are so different than traveling through a valley. Mountains and hills require you to climb instead of walking. There is also more equipment needed to even attempt to climb a huge hill or mountain. There is a lot of danger involved in mountain climbing because you could slip at any time and get seriously injured or die. And on the mountain of life I know I'm not the only one that has slipped while trying to climb some of the mountains of life.

Think about what happens when we slip, we fall. When we fall we get hurt, embarrassed, and discouraged. So somewhere between dusting ourselves off, picking rocks out of our flesh and cleaning our wounds we still have to find the strength to go on. We have to find strength to keep on climbing. We have to find the courage to find another foothold and another handgrip so we can lift our head and move upward once again.

I speak from experience because I failed so many times in my life. I've busted my lip, scarred my knees, broken bones, busted my head, injured my back and even threw in my towel to give up. But something down inside lead me to go back, pick up my towel, wipe the sweat from my head, wipe the tears from my eyes and try again.

Trying again takes so much inner strength, you have to swallow your pride and humble yourself to do so. Fear will overshadow you and whisper in your ear "you can't make it". Fear will say "you remember what happened last time". Fear will call you a fool while laughing in your face. I know, I've been there. I am filled with ideas and dreams that I never pursued. I've written three books but this is the first one to be published all because fear robbed me of stepping out on faith.

Now that I have overcome so many hills and mountains in my life I can now see that all was not lost. I can see that I receive strength, wisdom, courage, stability and knowledge. I'm stronger, I'm wiser, I'm better, so much better. When I look back over all the mountains God has brought me over I realize that it was worth all the hurt, pain, and hard work.

The struggles of climbing and falling build me up where I was torn down and strengthened me where I was weak. I now feel like I can go on even on my worst days. I'm now able to love the sunshine, respect the rain, enjoy the snow and yield to the thunderstorms that come in life.

So my words to anyone struggle in life right now. Never give up, keep on climbing in spite of how hard it gets. I remember the movie "Pursuit of Happiness". In the movie Will Smith plays the part of a man named Chris Gardner who struggled a long time trying to become somebody. He wanted to be somebody his son could trust and depend on. He lost his home, car, wife and his pride. Through all his endeavor to try to become successful he failed. He failed climbing mountains of rejection, frustration, anxiety, depression, poverty and low self-esteem. He dealt with all of this while attempting to provide for his son.

About mid-way through the movie he is so frustrated that he takes it out on his son. They were playing basketball. His son said, "I'm going Pro." But he looks at his son and says, "you probably wouldn't make it in basketball". He felt his son couldn't make it in basketball because he himself was only average. He quickly realized that he was wrong as he watched his son stop playing and put his basketball in his bag. He looked at this son and said, "If you have a dream, don't let anyone tell you that you can't do something". He goes on to say, "not even me", meaning that sometimes we can let parents keep us from pursuing our dreams.

Over the years many children have become discouraged by their negative, ignorant parents. Parents that were afraid of their child to play sports, be a police officer, or be in the military because the parents were afraid.

Why do parents have a right to hinder a child from an opportunity to pursue happiness?

So, parents should be very careful not to be quick to say what their child can't do. Be careful to not measure their child's future based on what they couldn't accomplish in their life. Remember, God's plan for your child may not be the same plans he had for you.

I remember in 1991 a movie came out called "The Five Heartbeats". In this movie five guys put together a singing group. Most of the guys parents didn't really support the singing group but one particular parent stood out the most. The lead singer, Eddie Caine's dad was so negative that Eddie struggled every day. After their first big show he was so happy in spite of the fact that his weren't there. He came home happy and his parents were outside. His dad walked up to him not to congratulate him but to say "you ain't @$!%, ain't gonna be @$!%, cause I ain't @$!%".

So he told his son that he was nothing, wasn't going to be nothing because he didn't become anything in life but a drunk. He had only become an abusive alcoholic so his son couldn't make it in music.

All I'm saying is make sure we encourage our children because the sky is the limit. Knowing that the sky is the limit we, as well as our kids, should have a mindset to never give up. I remember in elementary school there was a poster on the wall. The poster had a large pelican attempting to eat a frog. The whole body of the frog was in the pelican's mouth but the frog had one arm out of the pelican's mouth choking the pelican.

See, many people looked at that picture and laughed because at the top of the picture in big writing it said "Never Give Up".

As humorous as it seems, there was a message in the picture. You may look at that picture and laugh but the joke wasn't on the frog, the joke was on the pelican. What I mean is this: on the picture the pelican had a small neck and the frog's hand was completely around the pelican choking him severely. So my point is this, the frog may be in the pelican's mouth but the pelican can't swallow the frog because his little neck is being severely squeezed. So if the frog never gives up the pelican will pass out or die…if the frog never gives up!

I see it that the pelican represents the harsh world we live in. It seems to be attempting to swallow us up. It seems like we will be eaten alive but if we can get a grip on life, and keep a strong grip on life without giving up we can live. We can overcome this world and all of its trials and tribulation. Think about it this way, which creature is stronger in this picture? Everyone should answer the same way by saying: The pelican!

Nevertheless my answer is the frog.

I know that sounds stupid because the frog is so much smaller than the pelican and the frog is completely in the pelican's mouth. I know, but listen! The pelican has a will to eat but the frog has a will to live! It's hard to kill something that has a strong will to live. Anyone or anything with this mindset only gets knocked down but not knocked out. They get distracted but not destroyed. This is because through it all they always seem to find a way.

Remember for a moment there were two TV series that came on weekly, one was called McGyver and the other was the A-Team. Both shows had the same symbolic meanings. They always found themselves in some kind of trouble but they always found a way to get out of it. They would get locked in barns or in an abandoned building but they would always find odds and ends to create bombs, tools, or something to escape.

We should have this mindset when life has our backs against the wall, when life traps us, when life locks us up. We should be able to look all around us and search deep within and find some way to get loose again. I know it's not easy but I do know it's possible. Most of all I know it's an uphill climb!

About the Author

The author of this book is a simple everyday young man that made so many mistakes in his life. He didn't understand at the time that having a seizure, getting run over by a car, getting cut, shot at, getting arrested, having many car wrecks, becoming an alcohol and drug addict, involved in gang violence would one day lead to a better place. But then one day he met a man named Jesus that had to knock him down and literally prove to him that God was real and could do anything but fail.

Laurel Rose Publishing

Laurel Rose Publishing is a small publishing company located in North Mississippi. The company was created as a way for unknown authors to get published and get help in marketing their works. If you are interested in publishing a book and want to know how you can do so for FREE contact us at www.laurelrosepublishing.com.

Other Books by Laurel Rose Publishing

Fiction:

Finding Christmas by Ian Johnstone & Chad R Martin

Inspirational:

An Inspired Life by Lisa Cockrell

Scriptural Thoughts by Rev Raymond Cross

Why Am I So Happy? by Dr Mike Cockrell

Children's Books:

Our Family by Katie, Ariana, and Chad Martin

Silas' Fall Adventure by Dr Mike & Lisa Cockrell

The Prized Tooth by Prentis Goodwin

The Adventures Of Shawn Shaw Karate Baby by Auntie M

Dad Made A Mess by Shirley Rena Smith

Don't Color On The Wall (Growing with Chloe) by Shirley Rena Smith

Loralai The Lonely by Chad R Martin & Howard Boling

Stanley's Lost Gift by Chad R Martin & Howard Boling

Health & Wellness:

Simply Weight Loss by Dr Mike Cockrell

"My Successful Journey" Smoke Free in 14 Days or Less by Hope Crago

Rash Decision Making by Hope Crago

Biographies/Autobiographies:

Suffering For Victory by J.B. Jones

How To:

5 Keys To Publishing On Kindle by Chad Martin & Dr Mike Cockrell

Nature, Gardening, Landscaping:

The Hummer Garden by Lisa Cockrell

Safety:

Life Saving Tips by Hope Crago

Plays:

My Plays: Everyone Should Smile Every Now and Then by James Earl Smith

Poetry:

Treasures of The Heart by James Earl Smith

Stepping Forward: Exploring Nature and the World Through Haiku by James Earl Smith

Wisdom At The Foot of The Mountain by James Earl Smith

Avant 365 by Arthur Avant

The Art of Love by Arthur Avant

Hell's Castaway by Howard Boling

Reaching For The Horizon by James Earl Smith

Searching For The Eagle's Whereabouts by James Earl Smith

A Random Spread of Bones by Howard Boling

Young Writer's Series:

The Apple Thief by The Boys & Girls Club of Northwest Mississippi

Comics/Graphic Novels:

Dynamic Sequence Volume 1 by Nick King

Comedy:

Pooping Scared by Chad R Martin

Audio Books:

The Hummer Garden by Lisa Cockrell

Scriptural Thoughts by Rev. Ray Cross

www.ingramcontent.com/pod-product-compliance
Lightning Source LLC
Chambersburg PA
CBHW060942040426
42445CB00011B/964